T0113340

Kene D. Ewulu, Ed.D.

CHRIST-LED
REBOUND SERIES
—— BAD HABITS ——

WESTBOW
PRESS®
A DIVISION OF THOMAS NELSON
& ZONDERVAN

Scripture taken from the King James Version of the Bible.

Revised Standard Version of the Bible, copyright ©1952 [2nd edition, 1971] by the Division of Christian Education of the National Council of the Churches of Christ in the United States of America. Used by permission. All rights reserved.

This book is a work of non-fiction. Unless otherwise noted, the author and the publisher make no explicit guarantees as to the accuracy of the information contained in this book and in some cases, names of people and places have been altered to protect their privacy.

WestBow Press books may be ordered through booksellers or by contacting:

WestBow Press
A Division of Thomas Nelson & Zondervan
1663 Liberty Drive
Bloomington, IN 47403
www.westbowpress.com
1 (866) 928-1240

Because of the dynamic nature of the Internet, any web addresses or links contained in this book may have changed since publication and may no longer be valid. The views expressed in this work are solely those of the author and do not necessarily reflect the views of the publisher, and the publisher hereby disclaims any responsibility for them.

Any people depicted in stock imagery provided by Thinkstock are models, and such images are being used for illustrative purposes only. Certain stock imagery © Thinkstock.

ISBN: 978-1-5127-3791-2 (sc)
ISBN: 978-1-5127-3790-5 (e)

Library of Congress Control Number: 2016906136

Print information available on the last page.

WestBow Press rev. date: 04/13/2016

Contents

Author's Note

In my first book, titled *Christ-Led Rebound Principles: Sustaining Christian Deliverance and Victory*, life's issues that we struggle with were identified, scripturally backed solutions were proffered, and ways of keeping our victory were outlined.

I have, however, realized that modern Christians and non-Christians seldom read large amounts of print due to the proliferation of audio and video mediums of presentation. Readers want smaller booklets that deal with their particular and respective struggles. In essence, someone struggling with separation and divorce may not necessarily want to learn how to deal with the scourge of unemployment or depression. The Lord has therefore led me to break up the original book into small booklets. The first publication dealt with rebounding from inactivity and addressed action steps embrace to be delivered from inactivity and live free, victorious lives in Christ.

This second publication of the *Christ-Led Rebound Series* addresses bad habits. It will define and describe bad habits, proffer scripturally backed solutions for jettisoning them, and outline strategies to help retain our victory over them.

Carefully and prayerfully read this booklet, meditate on its contents, and put into practice all you will learn concerning recovery from bad habits.

I urge you afterward to step up, step over, shun bad habits, embrace good habits, and begin to live right by the grace and strengthening of our Lord Jesus Christ and the Holy Spirit of God!

The thief cometh not, but for to steal, and to kill, and to destroy: I am come that they might have life, and that they might have it more abundantly. (John 10:10 KJV)

Dedication

To my late parents, Godwin and Theodora, for teaching your children the value of good habits, hard work, honesty, and contentment, and for discouraging indolence and double speak!

It has been a while since you both went home to the Lord, but the lessons you taught us about good and bad habits still resound to your third generation.

Rest well!

—Dr. Kene D. Ewulu

Preamble

Actions and thoughts that we practice all the time become habitual and ingrained in us. When those habits conform to socially acceptable behavioral patterns and yield positive outcomes, they can be referred to as good habits.

On the other hand, when our habits lead to unacceptable behavior and yield negative outcomes, they can be classified as bad habits. In the world we live in today, society has begun to accept certain biblically unacceptable practices as okay due to the expansion of the definition of a person's rights and freedoms of expression and behavior.

Scenarios such as those listed in Galatians 5:19–21 are no longer frowned upon by modern society: adultery, fornication, lasciviousness, idolatry, witchcraft, hatred, variance, emulations, wrath, strife, seditions, heresies, envy, drunkenness, reveling, etc. Men and women have become desensitized to these ills, actively participating in some of them, viewing them as tolerable, or turning a blind eye so as not to be labeled "politically incorrect."

These practices, and others like them, have become habits for a lot of people—bad habits!

This booklet will define bad habits, identify some examples that plague us in our daily lives, and proffer scripturally based, definite action steps that, if taken, will lead us into recovery. We will also itemize some things we need to practice (and some that we need to avoid) to retain our liberty from bad habits and sustain our victory in every area of our lives.

Defining Bad Habits

The work of redemption by our Lord Jesus, and the ensuing Christian walk of believers, is a constant spiritual battle that will neither abate nor end until Christ's triumphant second coming and eventual victory over Satan.

We are assured of victory in this spiritual battle if we faithfully read and dwell on God's Word and share its mysteries with our families, our friends, and the rest of humanity. When we form the bad habit of lethargy in reading the Bible, we open ourselves to the encroachment of the Devil in every aspect of our lives.

Our behavior patterns in isolated situations become habits, and bad habits do not glorify God. Unchecked venting of our frustrations at work and at home reveals anger and a lack of self-control; these do not encourage our coworkers and family members to emulate us and to seek to serve our God. Furthermore, our inability to

...treat to the comforting words of Scripture during both the smooth sailing and trying periods of our lives is an early indication of a lack of faith. By neglecting to confess God's Word in and out of season, we not only fall prey to walking by sight, but we also discourage any onlookers, such as our non-Christian friends, from accepting Jesus as Lord and Savior.

> Ye are the salt of the earth: but if the salt have lost his savour, wherewith shall it be salted? it is thenceforth good for nothing, but to be cast out, and to be trodden under foot of men. Ye are the light of the world. A city that is set on an hill cannot be hid. Neither do men light a candle, and put it under a bushel, but on a candlestick; and it giveth light unto all that are in the house. Let your light so shine before men, that they may see your good works, and glorify your Father which is in heaven. (Matthew 5:13–15 KJV)

What are people saying and doing around you? Are your non-Christian friends and relatives careful about their behavior and language while in your company or in your home? Christians who allow filthy conversation in whatever gathering they find themselves are guilty of this bad habit, and it can lead to derision of our holy God. It is therefore expedient for us to let the light of God in us shine, more so when we are in unfamiliar congregations.

In our professional and secular lives, there may be gray areas where Christians lapse, such as the acceptance of bribery in the form of monetary coercion, the passive acceptance of the sublime violation of the rights of the "underdog," and the reluctance to accept and undo our mistakes. In doing these things, we don't allow the light of God to shine, and we encourage bad habits. These "small" deviations from God and his stipulated instructions soon become common practice and the way things are done. Sooner rather than later, they lead to the quietening of the Holy Spirit's still, small voice in our hearts.

My definition and description of bad habits are encapsulated in the following:

- Bad habits are negative feelings, actions, or inactions that we experience or engage in on a frequent basis.

- Bad habits include everything we do in private that, if done in public, would not glorify God, would bring shame to us, would cause rejection from godly society, and would lead others to live sub-optimally.
- Bad habits include the following: anger, lack of consideration, dishonesty, violence, meanness, jealousy, gossip, lies, drug and alcohol use, illicit sexual activity (pornography, masturbation, voyeurism, premarital sex, and sex with someone other than your spouse), and filthy conversation.
- Bad habits entrench us on the wrong path and derail our desire to live in a holy manner.

Rebounding from Bad Habits

> For God so loved the world, that he gave his only begotten Son, that whosoever believeth in him should not perish, but have everlasting life. (John 3:16 KJV)

Rebounding from bad habits can be achieved by following certain practical steps. These steps require personal discipline and dedication.

- Keep your mind focused on the positive side of things.
- Do not do anything you would not want done to you.
- Protect your relationships by being honest and considerate and by resisting anger.
- See yourself as an ambassador of Christ, and do not be involved in things Jesus would frown at. Do those things Jesus expects from his followers.

- Surround yourself with men and women of like mind, people whose actions and thoughts only strive to please God.

We will now look at these practical steps in greater detail. We will examine each of these strategies more comprehensively, identify supporting Scriptures for them, and look at how to make these steps work personally for us.

1. Keep your mind focused on the positive side of things.

We are what we think!

Thoughts always lead to belief and then action. If we therefore think good and positive thoughts about our situations and relationships, it is reasonable to assume that our subsequent actions will be in synch with those thoughts. They will lead to healthy situations.

The Bible warns us about this: "For as he thinketh in his heart, so is he" (Proverbs 23:7 KJV).

If we are what we think, it is only logical that to be successful we need to think as successful people, to be pure we need to think pure thoughts, and to be noble we need to think noble thoughts.

Another Bible verse that supports this train of thought declares the following:

> Finally, brethren, whatsoever things are true, whatsoever things are honest, whatsoever things are just, whatsoever things are pure, whatsoever things are lovely, whatsoever things are of good report; if there be any virtue, and if there be any praise, think on these things. (Philippians 4:8 KJV)

Stay focused on the positive; bad thoughts and their accompanying bad habits will be minimized!

2. Do not do anything you would not want done to you.

Everyone wants to be treated fairly, truthfully, and respectfully! We dream that our desires and expectations from others should be fulfilled.

In a perfect world, we want to receive good things from others. The Bible tells me that in order for that to happen, we must first be a blessing to others.

> Judge not, and ye shall not be judged: condemn not, and ye shall not be condemned: forgive, and ye shall be forgiven: Give, and it shall be given unto you; good measure, pressed down, and

> shaken together, and running over, shall men give into your bosom. For with the same measure that ye mete withal it shall be measured to you again. (Luke 6:37–38 KJV)

This goes to show that if we expect good things from other people, we must first be good to others in need. Jesus supports this statement by advising his audience the following:

> Therefore all things whatsoever ye would that men should do to you, do ye even so to them: for this is the law and the prophets. (Matthew 7:12 KJV)

When we obey these commands, then the promises of God become reality for us.

> For every one that asketh receiveth; and he that seeketh findeth; and to him that knocketh it shall be opened. (Matthew 7:8 KJV)

In a nutshell, we should do things for others that we expect them to do for us. We should work hard and extend kindness, consideration, and tactfulness to everyone we interact with.

- *We should give or lend willingly.* Others will do so for us too.

- *We should be understanding and nonjudgmental.* Others will forgive us and not judge us for our past or current mistakes.

- *We should not lie or gossip about others.* Others will not defame our character or malign us behind our backs.

- *We should work for others as if we are working for God.* Diligence and hard work eventually pay off; they showcase us as good workers. Promotions will eventually come to us from within and from the outside. God promises that a diligent person shall commune with influential people (Proverbs 22:29 paraphrased).

3. Protect your relationships by being honest and considerate and by resisting anger.

When we develop our reputations as honest, truthful persons, our relationships are strengthened due to enhanced trust! Keeping silent when we are provoked to anger also helps in maintaining existing good relationships.

keeping with this understanding, the book of wisdom advises this:

> He that handleth a matter wisely shall find good: and whoso trusted in the Lord, happy is he. Pleasant words are as a honeycomb, sweet to the soul and health to the bones. (Proverbs 16:20, 24 KJV)

We should therefore embrace good habits by:

- being honest, loving, and tactful;
- handling our issues with wisdom; and
- correcting others pleasantly, bringing healing and not strife with our corrective words or actions.

The Bible supports this advice by declaring, "A soft answer turneth away wrath: but grievous words stir up anger" (Proverbs 15:1 KJV).

Therefore, let us watch our tongues!

4. See yourself as an ambassador of Christ, and do not be involved in things that Jesus would frown at; do those things Jesus expects from his followers.

See yourself as holy. You are, after all, washed clean by Jesus' blood! Then become the ambassador you have been made to be, reconciling warring factions, loving everyone, and most importantly, praying for them. Supporting these assertions, three Scriptures readily come to mind.

Reminding us of our new standing with God:

> For thou art an holy people unto the Lord thy God: the Lord thy God hath chosen thee to be a special people unto himself, above all people that are upon the face of the earth. (Deuteronomy 7:6 KJV)

This Scripture reminds us of our ambassadorial position:

> Now then we are ambassadors for Christ, as though God did beseech you by us: we pray you in Christ's stead, be ye reconciled to God. (2 Corinthians 5:20 KJV)

This Scripture guides us on what we must do as people who have been set apart and who represent God and his Christ here on earth:

But I say unto you, Love your enemies, bless them that curse you, do good to them that hate you, and pray for them which despitefully use you, and persecute you. (Matthew 5:44 KJV)

In a nutshell, grace and good standing before God were freely given to us; let us humbly bring others to Jesus by doing the following:

- embracing who we are in Christ, holy by the grace of God
- fixing our personal relationship with God
- loving everyone, regardless of whether they deserve our love or how they feel about us

Let us walk away from bad habits and embrace good habits by relating well with God, staying holy, and treating others with consideration and understanding. We must always remember that we may be the only "Jesus" other people might ever encounter.

Representing Jesus means treating others right!

5. Surround yourself with men and women of like mind—people whose actions and thoughts only strive to please God.

Interact with others such as yourself, who have the same values—the fear of God. We are reminded of the importance of appropriate company:

> Iron sharpens iron; so a man sharpens the countenance of his friend. (Proverbs 27:17 KJV)

We should keep away from negative company, while gravitating to those who will encourage us to read and think on the Bible frequently; this strategy will yield lasting dividends. A widely read portion of the Bible declares this:

> Blessed is the man Who walks not in the counsel of the ungodly, Nor stands in the path of sinners, Nor sits in the seat of the scornful; But his delight is in the law of the Lord, And in His law he meditates day and night. He shall be like a tree Planted by the rivers of water, That brings forth its fruit in its season, Whose leaf also shall not wither; And whatever he does shall prosper. (Psalm 1:1–3 KJV)

As we absent ourselves from ungodly, scornful, or sinful company, and instead spend time in reading and meditating on God's Word, as well as in interacting with God-fearing people, we are to expect good social, physical, financial, and emotional wealth.

This means that we should do the following:

- interact with godly, supportive people
- positively influence negative people through prayer, godly advice, and good behavior
- stay away from obstinately negative people who might frustrate you or cause you to retrogress in your relationship with Christ
- Joyfully search and study the Bible frequently.

Think and act on the truths of the Bible, and "let it guide your thoughts, words, and actions continually" (Psalms 19:14 paraphrased). Habits form through sustained practices; we minimize bad habits and grow new, good habits if we are able to focus on positive things, do unto others as we would want them to do unto us, be honest and considerate, resist anger, be good ambassadors of Christ, and surround ourselves with like-minded people.

Practice makes perfect.

Victory through Good Habits

Jesus has a response for us as we battle anger, lack of consideration, dishonesty, violence, meanness, jealousy, gossip, lies, drugs, alcohol, illicit sexual activity, and filthy conversation. He says the following:

> Come unto me, all ye that labor and are heavy laden, and I will give you rest. Take my yoke upon you, and learn of me; for I am meek and lowly in heart: and ye shall find rest unto your souls. For my yoke is easy, and my burden is light. (Matthew 11:28-30)

In order to be practitioners of good habits, we must accept, embrace, and submit to Jesus. By rejecting bad habits and arising from the dust, we will see our mountains leveled, overcome our challenges, and become successful in our lives and ventures.

A few practical steps to retaining good habits are: reading the Bible frequently, being accountable to a mature Christian friend, being considerate, tactful, honest, and hardworking, loving others without reservation, and always praying and believing.

1. Reading the Bible frequently

> Thy Word have I hid in mine heart, that I might not sin against thee. (Psalm 119:11 KJV)

The Holy Bible is the infallible Word of God; it is also the Sword of the Spirit. The Holy Bible instructs us on what to do, reveals past successes and mistakes of others, imbues us with wisdom for life's situations, wins the victory for us, and cleanses us from within.

It is therefore critical that we study the Bible as often as we can. We, however, lead very busy lives and find ourselves relegating this task to the background. I have found that the advent of technology allows me to download an audio version of the Bible on my smartphone or tablet, and to listen to its contents in the background as my day progresses. I sometimes do this even when I am asleep and find that just like with computers, it has the ability to clean my spirit man up even while I rest. The Word of God is spiritual food for our souls and has the capability, as it is embedded into our hearts, of banishing our sinful thoughts, poor actions, and bad habits and enabling us to truly live holy before God!

2. Being accountable to a mature Christian friend

Choosing a mature Christian friend to be accountable to, to pray with, and to receive advice from when we are tempted to revert to our old ways is another way to reject bad habits.

> Two are better than one; because they have a good reward for their labor. For if they fall, the one will lift up his fellow: but woe to him that is alone when he falleth; for he hath not another to help him up. Again, if two lie together, then they have heat: but how can one be warm alone? And if one prevail against him, two shall withstand him; and a threefold cord is not quickly broken. (Ecclesiastes 4:9–12 KJV)

It is strengthening to have a trusted friend to lean on during trying times. It gets easier to withstand temptations and to pick oneself up should one fall. It is also more effective when we fight together and in unity. The Bible tells me, "One person would put one thousand foes to flight, but two people would put ten thousand foes to flight" (Deuteronomy 32:30 paraphrased). The increase of our effectiveness is exponentially greater when we collaborate with another person and fight as a unified group.

3. Being considerate and tactful

One good habit to nurture is being considerate of others in all things. When relating to other people, consider their sensitivities and only say or do those things that may affirm, encourage, or stabilize them. Think of their feelings or expectations, and try not to trample on them. Furthermore, when the truth needs to be told, do it in a gentle, tactful manner so that anger and resentment do not flare up. To buttress my argument, the book of wisdom declares the following:

> A soft answer turneth away wrath: but grievous words stir up anger. The tongue of the wise useth

knowledge aright: but the mouth of fools poureth out foolishness. (Proverbs 15:1–2 KJV)

When you are a subordinate, remember that bosses also benefit from considerate and tactful words and can grant you favor for choosing gentle words. Therefore, we should do the following:

> Honor all men. Love the brotherhood. Fear God. Honor the king. Servants, be subject to your masters with all fear; not only to the good and gentle, but also to the forward. (1 Peter 2:17–18 KJV)

Honest praise and gentle rebuke equate to consideration and tact and are good habits to form and nurture.

4. Being honest

Having an honest reputation builds up our integrity and opens doors for great and lasting relationships with others. Calling things as they are and refusing to alter the truth because of potential gains is a good habit that will also draw others to our God. Peter advises those who expect to live long and fruitfully:

> For he that will love life, and see good days, let him refrain his tongue from evil, and his lips that they speak no guile. (1 Peter 3:10 KJV)

God blesses those who prove themselves honest and above reproach. It might seem as if telling the truth in your situation would negatively impact your position, but speak the truth anyway, and watch God supernaturally alter your situation for your good. Choose the truth over a lie; choose the good over evil; and choose God over the Devil. Honor God with truth; He will honor you also:

> Lying lips are abomination to the Lord: but they that deal truly are his delight. (Proverbs 12:22 KJV)

Honesty equates to righteousness, and nations are blessed because honest people dwell there.

> Righteousness exalteth a nation: but sin is a reproach to any people. (Proverbs 14:34 KJV).

Build habitual honesty; your fortunes will blossom.

5. Working hard

God has promised to bless the work of our hands; our hands must therefore have work to do. We need to develop the good habit of working hard consistently and with the right perspective—for God. Diligence is extolled in the Bible:

> Seest thou a man diligent in his business? he shall stand before kings; he shall not stand before mean men. (Proverbs 22:29 KJV)

Consistently working hard toward your goals will ultimately bring you recognition through acknowledgments from influential people.

> Whatsoever thy hand findeth to do, do it with thy might; for there is no work, nor device, nor knowledge, nor wisdom, in the grave, whither thou goest. (Ecclesiastes 9:10 KJV)

> And whatsoever ye do, do it heartily, as to the Lord, and not unto men. (Colossians 3:21–22 KJV)

Diligently performing our tasks enthusiastically (whether our bosses are physically present or not) is a divine command that, if obeyed, shows our understanding that we actually work for God.

Make hard work your good habit, and prosper.

6. Loving others unconditionally

Choosing to cherish others irrespective of the warmth of the prevailing relationship is another good habit we should embrace. Jesus commands us to love:

> A new commandment I give unto you, That ye love one another; as I have loved you, that ye also love one another. (John 13:34 KJV)

This commandment is critical to our being able to relate to others, even when they have failed us. The Bible supports our loving unconditionally:

> And above all things have fervent charity among yourselves: for charity shall cover the multitude of sins. (1 Peter 4:8 KJV)

Love is a choice, and when we choose to love, we are not only fulfilling the law of God but increasing the self-esteem of others and the reciprocity of goodness that occurs when people do not feel judged for past mistakes. Love's characteristics are described thus:

> Love is patient and kind; love is not jealous or boastful; it is not arrogant or rude. Love does

not insist on its own way; it is not irritable or resentful; it does not rejoice at wrong, but rejoices in the right. Love bears all things, believes all things, hopes all things, endures all things. (1 Corinthians 13:4–7 RSV)

When you decide to extend love to someone, you have to do it with patience and understanding that you will have to remain charitable for as long as it takes. You will have to submit to the person, be happy in doing what is right, endure unpalatable situations, hope on your ideals, and always give the other person the benefit of the doubt!

Love is the greatest gift we can give another person!

7. Praying and Believing Always

We are enjoined to pray frequently and to believe without wavering! Prayer is two-way communication with God; it requires that we communicate back and forth with God about our needs. There is therefore a time to ask and a time to listen for God's response. This is prayer in action. We are advised to pray all the time:

Pray without ceasing. (1 Thessalonians 5:17 KJV)

After we make our requests known to God, it is important that we be thankful in advance for answers to our petitions and not fret about them anymore. After all, if God has your back, no one can undermine or defeat you:

> Be careful for nothing; but in everything by prayer and supplication with thanksgiving let your requests be made known unto God. (Philippians 4:6 KJV)

This Scripture underscores the importance of believing we have received as soon as we have prayed to God. It tells us to ask God with thanksgiving in our hearts because we know we will receive what we petitioned God for.

We are also to ask with utmost belief or faith. We are encouraged to ask without wavering. Otherwise our requests will not be granted (James 1:6–8 paraphrased). Let us resolve to seek God's face in prayer, believe we have received all we prayed for, be patiently expectant, and remember that God never fails, and neither is He ever late.

We are to pray in faith!

Epilogue

As an avid follower of tennis, I observed that tennis players are only as good as they are in practice! They train their muscles to repeatedly hit certain shots in a definite way; this ensures that in the heat of competitive matches, their muscles remember those swings and unconsciously repeat them. Tennis players therefore form certain habits (whether good or bad) and stick to them during competitions.

Likewise, what we do in private translates to the public. If we build good habits, they will be replicated in our public endeavors, often leading to successful ventures. On the other hand, if we indulge in bad habits, they will eventually transform into our default way of doing things and ultimately lead us to failure or scorn.

Let us resolve now to rebound from bad habits by renewing our minds; this gives us strength to overcome our fleshly emotions and walk in obedience to the calling of God. We must conform to God's will for our lives and allow the Word of God renew and transform us:

> And be not conformed to this world: but be ye transformed by the renewing of your mind, that ye may prove what is that good, and acceptable, and perfect, will of God. (Romans 12:2 KJV)

There are several excuses people make for retaining their bad habits. These range from the need to conform with a failing society, to the realization that others are getting away with these bad habits, to rebellion from moral and ethical authorities, to greed and avarice.

Fortunately, our newly acquired victory over bad habits can be sustained by saying no to temptation daily, remaining accountable to a mature Christian friend, staying vigilant in prayer and study of the Word of God, glorifying God, and continually depending on the Holy Spirit. Jesus comforts and strengthens us with this promise:

> My sheep hear my voice, and I know them, and they follow me: And I give unto them eternal

life; and they shall never perish, neither shall any man pluck them out of my hand. My Father, which gave them me, is greater than all; and no man is able to pluck them out of my Father's hand. (John 10:27–29 KJV)

When we persist on this journey from bad to good habits, God will crown our resolve and efforts with success. God promised He will never forsake us but will be with us through our mountaintop and valley experiences.

Do your bit therefore; trust God and thrive!

Glossary

Ambassador of Christ: Someone who professes Jesus Christ as his or her Lord and Savior. Non-Christians therefore perceive that person as an example of what a good Christian should be; they see the person as an ambassador who mirrors Christ's image and persona.

Bad Habits: Negative feelings, actions or inactions that we experience or engage in on a frequent basis. They include everything we do in private that, if done in public, will not glorify God, will bring shame to us, will cause rejection from godly society, or will cause others to live sub-optimally. Bad habits place us on the wrong path and fight our desire to live holy.

Christ-Led Rebound: The process of recovery from personal challenges. It incorporates biblical instructions, insight, encouragement, and prayers offered to God through His Son, Jesus Christ. It means complete dependence on the promises of Jesus Christ, that He will set us permanently and completely free, when we profess His lordship and obey foundational Christian beliefs.

Faith: Believing in God, and not doubting that whatever you have asked of Him has been given to you. This can also be extended, to a lesser extent, to others.

Love: Being charitable, empathetic, supportive, and encouraging to others. Emulating Jesus and placing others' needs ahead of ours. We love when we sacrificially give of our time, resources, and energy to others.

Meditate: To study deeply and take enough time to think on what one studied. It is advisable to pray for clarity and understanding before meditating on the Word of God.

Obedience: Following God's instructions, even when we do not understand the reasoning or logic behind them. God values obedience above so many things because we display our trust in Him when we obey Him without questioning.

Praise: Extolling God for the things He has done for us, or in other cases, for the things we believe He will yet do for us. God can be praised through our voices or by utilizing musical instruments.

Quiet Time: A time set aside for reading the Word of God, praying, or listening to/singing songs of praise to God.

Redemption: Buying back a debt from someone. It is a release from accountability or payment, with forgiveness and a new start. The blood of Jesus was shed on the cross, so all sinners (we all) are forgiven and redeemed from the clutches of the Devil. Believing that Jesus died for us also and accepting Him as Lord and Savior assures us of redemption and subsequently, salvation.

Rest: Complete faith in God. A place in our minds where we can relinquish every worry or anxiety and believe without any doubt that God will intervene for our good. The place where the peace of God that passes all understanding is experienced and enjoyed.

Righteousness: The desire to do what is right and acceptable before the eyes of God. This can actually translate into successfully living right before God, but God looks first at the intentions of the heart. Exhibiting and utilizing other fruits of the Spirit, such as faith, patience, self-control, gentleness, humility, etc., are virtues that God admires in us and that He can use as yardsticks for holy living or righteousness. Note that in order to resist the Devil and be righteous, we all need God's help and enablement.

Spiritual Battle: The fight between good and evil that rages on in the spiritual realm. Everything that happens to us in the physical first occurs in the spiritual. Our prayer to God is a spiritual battle; it precedes God's blessings, and that is why Jesus asked us to ask, seek, and knock, so we can receive, find, and have open doors. Spiritual battles will go on until Jesus Christ's triumphant second coming.

Unity: Agreeing on something together; this often leads to exceptional victories and even more so if we are in unity with God. Knowing God's will for a situation and aligning with His will depicts perfect unity.

Worship: A higher form of praise where we extol God for who He is and not necessarily for the things he has done for us. A scenario where we just want to be in his presence, and where we are not necessarily asking him for anything!

Yoke: Any challenge we face that might have emanated from the spiritual. Lying, greed, envy, and sexual immorality are examples of yokes that spring from the Devil. Jesus' yoke, however, is easy because he loves us, died for us, and ever lives to intercede for us in God the Father's presence. We are commanded to put on Jesus' yoke.

About the Author

Dr. Kene D. Ewulu is a professor of organizational leadership and project management, an ordained pastor, and author of the *Christ-Led Rebound Series*. He combines his academic pursuits with an empathetic heart for others, burning with the passion to enable men and women to embrace their mandates as spiritual leaders and moral compasses at home, at work, and in their communities.

Kene is the founder and vice president of the Caleb Assembly, a nonprofit Christian ministry based in Columbia, South Carolina. The Caleb Assembly facilitates seminars and retreats for churches, motivates people in halfway homes, and challenges others to rebound onto righteous living through periodic global newsletters.

He resides in Columbia with his wife, Ijeoma, and their three teenage children.

Contact

www.thecalebassembly.org

kdewulu@thecalebassembly.org

www.ReboundSeries.com

Other Publications

- *Christ-Led Rebound Principles: Sustaining Christian Deliverance and Victory*
- *Christ-Led Rebound Series: Inactivity*